THE DESERT WILL REJOICE
and blossom as the rose

VOLUME II
Bethel

THE STORY OF THE FULFILMENT OF THE
FINAL PART OF A
THREE-PART PROPHECY GIVEN IN 1987
ABOUT THE CITY OF BIRMINGHAM

Dr Christine Parkinson

Published by New Generation Publishing in 2024

Copyright © Christine Parkinson 2024

First Edition

The author asserts the moral right under the Copyright, Designs and Patents Act 1988 to be identified as the author of this work.

All Rights reserved. No part of this publication may be reproduced, stored in a retrieval system or transmitted, in any form or by any means without the prior consent of the author, nor be otherwise circulated in any form of binding or cover other than that which it is published and without a similar condition being imposed on the subsequent purchaser.

ISBN: 978-1-83563-432-5

www.newgeneration-publishing.com

New Generation Publishing

Author's Notes

This book contains quotations from the Bible. In each case, the translation from which the quotation has been taken is included, as an abbreviation, in brackets after the reference, as follows:

(LB) Holy Bible, New Living translation © Tyndale House Publishers, Inc., Wheaton, Illinois, 1996

(NIV) Holy Bible, New International Version ©1984 by International Bible Society. Used by permission of Hodder & Stoughton.

TABLE OF CONTENTS

FOREWORD vi

Introduction 1

Chapter 1 – Bethel - The Revelation 8

Chapter 2 – The Bethel Logo 13

Chapter 3 – Early Developments 18

Chapter 4 – The Development of the Doula Project 25

Chapter 5 – E's story 32

Chapter 6 – Other healthy living activities 36

Chapter 7 – Reversals 38

Chapter 8 – The Growth of Bethel 48

Chapter 9 – The Cairn Consortium 65

End Piece 68

FOREWORD

written by the Chairman of Bethel Health and Healing Network

I will never forget the first time I met Christine Parkinson. It was the evening of 14th July 2021. My introduction to Bethel was by way of joining the Rapha Listening service, responding to a call mainly due to the lack of male listeners back in the April of the same year. Previous to and leading up to this point, I had been dogged by my conscience over a period of time to stop talking about "giving back" and to actually do it. And now here I was on a zoom interview with Jacynth Ivey (then chair) Rosie Steer-Palmer (consultant) and Christine Parkinson (Bethel Founder/Trustee) being interviewed for the role of Chair. To say that I was interviewed within an inch of my life by these three women would have been an understatement, but they saw something in me (particularly Christine) that I'm not sure that I actually saw in myself.

However, what struck me in that interview was when Christine shared briefly, the visionary aspect of how Bethel (along with Jericho and Gilgal) had been birthed and realised over those many years. Having been a passionate Christian for over forty years and a Pastor for some of those years, I have not been devoid of witnessing and hearing of the mighty hand of God moving in mysterious and yes sometimes miraculous ways.

And yet here I was captivated by this story of the birth of Bethel. More was to come when, over time, I was able to spend some private and quality time over breakfasts and lunches (I do recommend Becketts Farm restaurant for either) with Christine, where I was able to gain further insight, not just into the journey of Bethel, but also the journey of this unassuming but very prayerfully astute and obedient woman of God.

After reading volume one of Christine's book 'The Desert will Rejoice', it gave me a personal drive to ensure that under my tenure as Chair of this beautiful Charity, the founding vision should never be lost or overcome by any outside influence or distraction. Having now read the sequel 'The Desert Will Rejoice volume two', my resolve is complete, as I am wholly convinced that God's hand has and continues to be firmly on this small charity (which punches way above its weight) as it continues to serve the community.

I have never met anyone like Christine, whose whole life revolves around a prayerful relationship with God, and as such, I have learned so much on my own specific journey of how key that is as a Christian, particularly in an age where there are many challenges and hurdles which can derail one's faith.

I mention these things to highlight that Christine is the real deal. That which she writes about, she lives with quiet passion, integrity and humility. I loved reading this book. Christine does not gloss over the struggles and painful times and indeed the seeming failures. Yet reading these pages I believe you will come away inspired, encouraged and filled with faith to pursue and trust our dependable yet unpredictable God (reversals) with all gusto!

Duncan Moore
Chair of Bethel Health & Healing Network

Introduction

In 1986, a Dutch pastor's wife, Maria Blom, received a prophecy, centred around a derelict building in Birmingham. The prophecy stated that this building would become a Christian project for women and children, to be called Gilgal. A further revelation given to her was that two other Christian projects would come after, to be named Jericho and Bethel. I did not know Maria at that time but I became involved when God spoke to me about the same derelict building (see later).

So, the establishment of Bethel Health and Healing Network forms the third part of the prophecy given to Maria Blom. The outcomes of the prophecy were written up and published by me in the first volume of "The Desert Will Rejoice." This first volume was published 20 years ago in 2004, when Bethel's journey had only just begun, so the first volume doesn't give the whole story of the early stages of establishing the Bethel vision. Many people have been asking me for the whole story, so this volume II attempts to give the complete story for Bethel, by filling in the details from 2004 to 2024.

People have said to me that the first book (Volume I) is inspirational; in fact one church used it for their Bible study sessions. God was certainly very much at work in Birmingham during the late eighties and into the millennium. The story of the development of the two preceding projects in the prophecy, Gilgal and Jericho, blows you away and I trust that the beginnings of the Bethel Health and Healing Network will do the same.

The story of the prophecy is in Volume I but the revelation and vision for Bethel was not given until March 2001, so Bethel's story will begin there in 2001. Of necessity, it is written in the first person, as an account of how I heard and witnessed events. Others might give a different story but this is written from the author's perspective.

Those early years were an amazing time of receiving revelations and pictures from God whilst at prayer. Some people who are not Christians, and even some who are Christians, have trouble in believing that God still speaks to us today, through revelations, visions, words and pictures. But my experience is that, the closer you are in your walk with God, and the more prayerful your life is, the more likely you are to receive such visions. This story is in two parts really: the visions that were given and the practical working out of setting up and funding a new project.

Not all Christians can hear God speaking, nor see God-given pictures and visions and some think that it is all part of an over-active imagination or even wishful thinking. One elderly pastor colleague, for whom I had a great deal of respect, a very committed Christian (now with the Lord, bless him), said that it all sounded rather "airy fairy" to him. But I hope that you'll bear with me as I write this story and I pray that you too will hear God speaking through these pages.

As an experienced scientist, I know that clear evidence and analysis is important when making decisions. But I also know, as a scientist, that keeping an open mind is also important and that some experiences in the godly realm are in a totally different dimension, that cannot be subjected to analytical scrutiny.

> *"For the foolishness of God is wiser than man's wisdom, and the weakness of God is stronger than man's strength."*
> 1 Cor.1:25 (NIV).

But, before I start the story, let me tell you something about my calling from God and how I came to be in Birmingham's inner city, so that you can have the whole story in context.

My testimony

I first gave my heart to Jesus when I was 8 years old and was baptised by full immersion when just 14 years old. At that young age, I believed that God wanted me to be a missionary and that I must first qualify as a doctor, so that I could add a medical dimension to the missionary work. However, in my teenage years, the enemy was very much at work to stop me from fulfilling this calling and I'm sorry to say that I stopped applying for a place at medical school, took a job in medical research when I left school, then married the wrong man when only 19 years old and, through his influence and the undermining of my calling, drifted away from the church and went to Australia.

The marriage became violent and I found myself being a victim of deliberate cruelty and sadism, with attempted strangulation, rape, attacks with knives, stamped on, burnt with lighted cigarettes, my clothing torn up - and constantly being verbally abused, wrongly accused and shouted at in a derogatory manner. I had no experience of this type of behaviour, growing up in my gentle, over-protective family, and I didn't know how to deal with it.

After three years of this abuse, I had to flee for my life when he tried to run me down with his car. I put as many miles as I could between myself and this psychopathic man as, in those days, there were no refuges for victims of domestic violence to flee to. For much of that frenzied escape, seeking safety, I was starving and homeless, sleeping under the stars in outback and coastal Australia.

Yet God was very gracious to me, providing me with supportive travelling companions in Australia, who helped me with my escape, on a long journey south from Darwin, across the central outback, then over to the Queensland coast and down the east coast of Australia to Sydney.

Later, the means was provided for me to return home to England with my infant son, where there were opportunities to study again and to resume work in medical research. Thus, I began to rebuild my life.

In 1976, when in my early thirties, I had a life-changing and powerful experience of God. Whilst walking alone at dawn in an empty forest, I suddenly felt God's holiness surrounding me; indeed, the very ground on which I was standing felt like holy ground. During this encounter, God spoke to me, giving me guidance for the future, with the words, "Keep your eyes on me and the way for your life will become clear." The story of this experience is described fully in the first chapter of my first book, "I Will Lift up my Eyes." It was the beginning of a patient God gradually drawing me back to himself.

Not long after this, whilst in church one Sunday morning, I felt God was calling me to devote the rest of my life to serving the poor, the marginalised and those in great need. "I want to do that, God," I whispered. "But where do I start?" His reply was surprising. "Just obey me," he said.

"Those who obey his commands live in him, and he in them. And this is how we know he lives in us: we know it by the Spirit he gave us."
1 John 3:24 (NIV).

Obedience didn't come easily to me in those days but these words led me into studying God's Word more deeply, to listening for his voice in prayer and to eventually leaving behind my medical research work in London and moving to Birmingham in 1984. I was led to Small Heath Baptist Church, where I was welcomed and received with respect. I received the anointing of the Holy Spirit, as well as Christian healing for many of the traumas I had been through earlier in my life.

God's call to work in Birmingham's inner city came in 1987, when I was appointed as Urban Missioner to 12 inner city Baptist churches, one of which was the church where I worshipped (Small Heath Baptist Church). Another of these 12 churches was Edward Road Baptist in Balsall Heath, whose pastor had the vision to develop a training centre, which later became the Jericho Centre. So, two of these 12 churches became involved in setting up projects helping the poorest of the poor and the most marginalised people in the city, projects that fulfilled the prophecy given to Maria Blom.

My involvement in the three prophetic projects started like this:

In 1987, I heard an audible voice whilst I was driving along an inner-city main road, near my church. The voice urgently said, "That's the Place!" I looked across and saw a derelict building and **that place**, which I was driving past, eventually became a refuge for abused women, through some miraculous interventions and financial provision from God. He was so gracious in involving me in setting up the women's refuge, to help women who had been through similar experiences to my own.

The Gilgal Refuge was the first of three prophetic projects, whose development is described in my second book, "The Desert Will Rejoice." And this final story, of Bethel's development, follows on as Volume II of "The Desert Will Rejoice," Bethel being the name given to the third part of Maria Blom's original prophecy, when she described it to us. The three prophecy projects, as I call them now, are up and fully functioning; the first two have recently celebrated their 30th anniversaries. They also work together in developing new initiatives through a consortium, the Cairn Consortium. More of this will be described towards the end of the book.

CEP

Chapter 1 – Bethel - The Revelation

How it all began

In 2001, I was praying with some friends from my church at their house in a cell group. We had been studying the Bible together, Matthew chapter 3, especially the story of the baptism of Jesus:

> *"As soon as Jesus was baptised, he went up out of the water. At that moment, heaven was opened, and he saw the Spirit of God descending like a dove and lighting on him. And a voice from heaven said, "This is my son, whom I love: with him I am well pleased."*
> Matt. 3: 16-17 (NIV)

In the house group, we discussed this Bible passage and what might have been meant by the words *"heaven was opened."* Following the Bible study, we had a time of worship and prayer – a time of waiting on God. As I rested in God's presence, I saw a picture in my mind of Jesus at his baptism, exactly as we had been reading in the Bible. It was an awe-inspiring picture. The room I was in was filled with brilliant light and angels were ascending and descending in that light. A dove was there, the Holy Spirit, mingling with the angels. At that moment, the heavens had been opened to me too and I felt God's presence in the room in such a powerful way.

The picture took my breath away. I was deeply affected by this vision and continued in prayer about it for several days, fasting and seeking its meaning for me. In my spiritual walk until then, I was aware that, in the Bible, God frequently accompanied a commissioning or revelation to different people with a vision of his glory (see Gen 28; Exodus 3 & 33:18-22; Isaiah 6; Ezekial 1; Dan10; Acts 9; Rev 1:9-18). And I had certainly seen God's glory – **and felt his presence**!

So, what did this mean for me now? And for my walk with the Lord?

After three days of fasting and prayer, it came to me as a sudden insight. The picture I had seen was similar to the one that Jacob had dreamed when fleeing from his family, after he had deceived them. It is described in Genesis 28:

"Jacob had a dream in which he saw a stairway resting on the earth with its top reaching to heaven, and the angels of God were ascending and descending on it. There above it stood the Lord."
Gen: 28, 12-13 (NIV).

Jacob believed that he had seen the Gate of Heaven in his dream and he named the place where he had this dream *"Bethel."*

After this insight, everything suddenly clicked into place for me! We had already been working on developing the first two parts of the prophecy – Gilgal and Jericho – and I knew that the final part of the prophecy was to be named *"Bethel,"* as originally shared by Maria Blom. Was God telling me that it was now time to develop Bethel?

Then, somewhere deep within me, I heard these words:

"Yes. The time is now right for the third part of the prophecy to take place – Bethel. It is to be a Christian Healing Centre and a Healthy Living Centre."

I was bowled over by this. And excited too! Maybe I would not have been so excited if I had known then that, over the next 20 years or so, there would be so many ups and downs in the full development of the Bethel vision – and that I would come close to giving up on it.

Volume I describes the next few months in the development and I will not repeat them here, just pick out a few things that have become significant for the journey to where Bethel is now at the start of 2024.

The first significant event happened during prayer with several different groupings of people in the early days. These people did not know each other, but they were giving me constant confirmation of the Bethel vision, through pictures they shared and Bible passages about cleansing water, fountains, streams and healing leaves. One person described a picture of people who were trapped in mud, who needed to be drawn out of it, to be cleansed with water from a sparkling stream. Other people were leaning over and drawing them out of the mud.

So we had confirmation that it was the time for Bethel over and over again. I was sure of this. The image of people being trapped in mud and needing to be pulled out of it and cleansed with clean water, really spoke to me.

I had wanted to be really sure that Bethel didn't duplicate other ministries that were already going on in the city and these confirmations of the vision showed me that we should proceed.

Chapter 2 – The Bethel Logo

So, how did Bethel come to choose a purple flower for its logo? The answer to this is that it came on two separate occasions, from different people. The first time was very early on, when we were encouraged, by Jackie, to see Bethel like a flower for the city. And, like a flower, it had a hub and spokes – a central project, the corona of the flower, but reaching out with satellite centres, like the petals and sepals of the flower.
A couple of years later somebody else saw a picture of a flower again. This time it was David, who was praying with the first Bethel steering group. He saw an image of a passion flower – a beautiful purple passion flower! David was overwhelmed by this picture, relating it to the Passion of Christ, and he was virtually brought to tears with the emotion that he felt when he saw the flower. And so Bethel's first chair, Graham Hartland, designed the first Bethel logo online as a passion flower.

The first Bethel passion flower logo

Later, in Bethel's development, the passion flower image was digitised, so that the current logo looks like this:

The current Bethel logo

The association of water with Bethel was also quite clearly going to be Living Water (John 4:10): the work of the Holy Spirit in cleansing and healing people of what had happened to them in the past.

I was not sure if I'd ever seen a passion flower, so I did a Wikipedia search on it. And I learnt that it is large and beautiful, pollinated by bees, wasps, bats, butterflies and even humming birds. There is a compound in its leaves and roots that has been used in traditional medicine for anxiety, depression or panic attacks. And I also learned that it produces fruits – passion fruits. And I had come across passion fruits before, when I lived in Australia in the 60s, and even had a job at one time, harvesting them for a farmer. The passion flower is also a vine and it has tendrils. And all of these characteristics give weight to what Bethel is all about:

- A beautiful flower in a dirty urbanised city;
- A central but rather unusual corona, the Bethel Centre, place of welcome, with beautiful petals reaching out into other places;
- A flower which provides sustenance (nectar to its pollinators – and sustenance to its client groups);
- A plant which produces fruits, which reminds me of the fruits of the Spirit: love, joy, peace, patience, kindness, goodness, faithfulness, gentleness and self-control (Gal 5: 22-23). Bethel's values.
- Part of a vine – John 15:1. "Jesus said: I am the true Vine and my father is the gardener." Jesus is central to the vision of Bethel.
- A vine with tendrils, reaching out to anchor it and to make it stable;
- Compounds in its leaves and roots that have been used in traditional medicine (Rev.22:2 the tree of life, with leaves for the healing of the nations).

But, some months into the development of the project, I received another powerful picture from the Lord, which combined the two together: the water and the flower. Whilst at prayer in my house group again, I felt God was placing something in my hands. It was a beautiful flower, with drops of dew on its petals and, as I looked at it, it grew in my hands to the size of a chalice and the drops of dew filled it up until it was flowing over with water. And people were coming up and drinking from the chalice and they were being healed and blessed with this Living Water.

**The flower in my hands turned into a chalice overflowing
with Living Water**

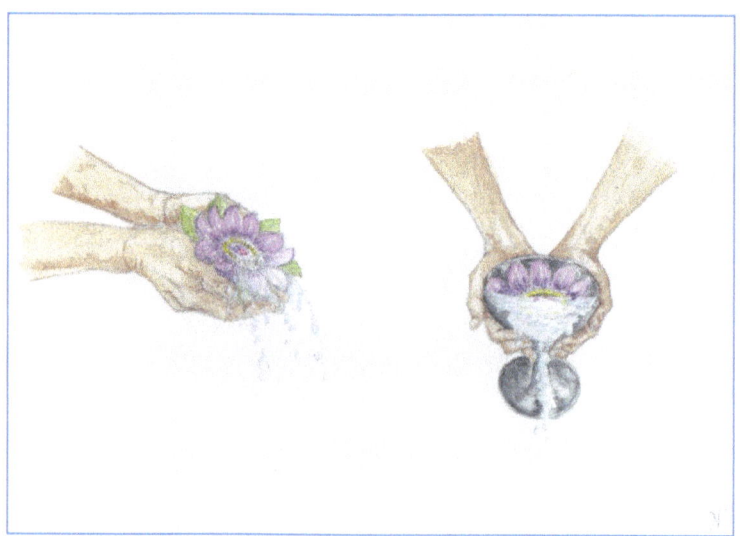

I have often wondered why in this vision I had been alone in holding the chalice of living water, for others were journeying with me at different times, to bring about the vision for Bethel. I didn't want to be the only person taking the vision forward but I have come to realise that there would be times when I would be alone in holding onto the vision, persevering and making sure it didn't die. That, in fact, God was affirming me as the vision-carrier, to encourage me to keep going when others left or didn't agree on the way forward.

Also, another Bible passage was used by God to encourage me during times when everything seemed to be lost:

> *"As the rain and the snow come down from heaven, and do not return to it without watering the earth and making it bud and flourish, so that it yields seed for the sower and bread for the eater,* **so is my word that goes out from my mouth: It will not return to me empty, but will accomplish what I desire and achieve the purpose for which I sent it.***"*
> Isaiah 55: 10-11 (NIV)

Chapter 3 – Early Developments

Three years after I first received the revelation for Bethel, I brought together a steering group of seven people in 2004, to take the vision forward, and most of this group eventually became trustees of the registered charity that was formed in 2006, with Graham Hartland as chair. The steering group put together a Statement of Purpose and a Statement of Faith.

> **Bethel Health and Healing Network**
>
> **Statement of Purpose**
>
> Bethel Health and Healing Network is a registered charity and a company limited by guarantee, established on Christian faith and principles. It aims to offer a range of services that will promote the health and well being of the disadvantaged people of Birmingham and its environs, by enabling them to maximise their physical, psychological and spiritual potential, through achieving balance and wholeness within themselves, their relationships and their community. People of all faiths, races and cultures are welcome, without any fear of discrimination, to the services we offer.

You will see from the statement of purpose, that it was clear from the beginning that the Bethel Health & Healing Network would be about helping all people who came to us, regardless of their faith, history, ethnicity and background. Whilst it was to be a Christian project, it was not to be restricted to Christians alone and nobody who came to the project would be excluded. From early in the project, Graham said that he felt his role was to help Bethel to set up a strong, stable framework under which it would operate, and he led the group, then Board, loyally for 8 years.

In 2007 two new people joined the project, a husband and wife, Tom and Mary. Tom became treasurer and company secretary of the charity and Mary, a nurse, wanted to develop a parish nursing ministry as a volunteer in Sparkbrook, under the Bethel umbrella. One of the trustees, Lynda, was very much into parish nursing too, so we embraced the concept. Many of the aims of parish nursing overlapped with the Bethel healthy living vision, so we journeyed together for a while.

Rooted in the Biblical concept of *shalom*, Parish Nursing operates by supporting people and communities towards the concept of whole-person healthcare, which is about the person's overall well-being, and includes spiritual, physical, mental and social aspects of health. All Parish Nurses are registered nurses and are appointed or employed through a local church or Christian organisation. Most of them continue in their work for the NHS, although some work solely as a Parish Nurse. See parish nursing website for further details: parishnursing.org.uk

At about the same time, we started to work in partnership with a local Anglican church, Christ Church, which owned a community house, Azadi House, as well as wanting to develop their large church site, near Farm Park in Sparkbrook, Birmingham. The church needed to be demolished and rebuilt; it had already been in a poor state of repair and was further damaged by the 2005 Birmingham tornado. This seemed an opportune time to build the Bethel Centre in partnership, alongside their new church and in partnership with them, on their large site. We started fundraising for this purpose, as well as doing door-to-door research in the Sparkbrook area, to establish the need and that local people, mainly of the Muslim faith, would be willing to use the healthy living activities that Bethel planned to offer, alongside the parish nursing initiative. We knew that Sparkbrook was within a circle of deprivation surrounding the city centre and that Census statistics had shown that there were significant health problems within this area. The door-to-door survey helped to confirm this.

When asked a general question about what facilities were missing in the area, one third of the local people mentioned a lack of exercise or sporting activities, ten per cent mentioned a lack of social activities and one in ten mentioned specific health support that was not available locally from the NHS. Just over half of households had within them at least one person who was not in good health and 80% of these said that it restricted their lives; conditions mentioned were diabetes (49%), physical disability (27.5%), learning disability (10%), heart disease (27.5%), asthma (23%), cancer, arthritis (36%), autism, dementia, ulcer, hypertension (64%), stroke (8.7%), mental illness (23%), addiction (4%), obesity (20%).

A list of 30 different services that Bethel might offer in the healthy living centre was given to the interviewees, to see whether they would use such services/ facilities if on offer. The following list gives the top 15 preferences from this list:

Keep fit (86%); Trips and outings away from the area (83%); Help with form-filling (81%); Personal health advice (78%); Groups for people with an illness in common (78%); Health information (77%); A drop-in facility (75%); Groups for the elderly (76%); Social activities (72%); Advocacy (72%); Somebody to talk through their problems with (counselling) (71%); Health Education (70%); Help with addictions eg smoking, alcohol, drugs (70%);

Women-only health sessions (69%); Youth Club (67%)

So, this small, local door-to-door survey established that there was a whole array of health-related activities that Bethel might develop in its proposed Healthy Living Centre in Sparkbrook.

As well as the parish nursing, Pauline, one of the trustees, a qualified Christian counsellor, started offering a counselling service at Azadi House. Several of the trustees also attended training in theophostic ministry, a new type of prayer ministry originating in the USA, in which, through prayer, God is invited to shine a light into the problems of the person being prayed for (theophostic, meaning God-light, or God bringing a light-bulb moment into that person's life). Pauline developed this to a new form of prayer ministry, which she called Safe Place Prayer ministry. Further information about theophostic ministry can be found in "Beyond Tolerable Recovery" by Ed M. Smith (1996); Alathia Publishing. This teaching is based on the premise that normal Christian prayer for an individual can make them feel better but that more in-depth techniques are required to deal with deep-seated issues and emotional wounding.

Isabella, one of the board members later introduced the Board to *Bethel Sozo Ministry*, which also came originally from the USA, and is practised by Harvest Ministries, in Hall Green, Birmingham UK. It teaches the package of tools used in this ministry for setting people free. Their statement says, *"Our aim is to love people and to provide information, so that the healing of past wounds can break strongholds, replace lies with truth and close doors to the enemy."*

We also began to hold healing services at various inner-city churches for people who sought prayer for the issues they were facing in life. Most of the board members at that time had experience in offering prayer ministry in their own churches, so we had the team to do this. Some people were really blessed by this ministry, though it never really took off at that time. Because we didn't have a building of our own, we used other churches for the healing services and it was difficult to promote locally the fact that healing services were taking place in these churches. Once Bethel Health & Healing Network establishes its own base, its vision is to offer one of these kinds of prayer ministry, to help people to be freed from long-standing issues relating to past traumas and issues arising from childhood.

Then Bethel had a setback, preventing the immediate development of any of the above, as there was a change of leadership in Christ Church, Sparkbrook and the new team chose to go in a different direction, by partnering with the NHS rather than Bethel. The outcome was that a huge NHS health centre was built on their former church site, and a smaller church was built opposite, to be based mainly in community outreach. There was no longer any room on the new church site for a Bethel Centre and the new Christ Church was too small to accommodate Bethel's team and plans. For a while, Bethel rented an office in the new NHS centre but it was very cramped, so we eventually moved elsewhere.

We kept going, despite this disappointment and received a small development grant, to help us to find a suitable building. After viewing three buildings, the favourite was a large former children's home in Highgate, Birmingham. Much time and effort was put into plans to adapt this building for Bethel's use. But, after lots of discussions and fundraising, we were unable to go ahead, as the owners had other plans for it.

We looked at so many different buildings at this time but nearly always they were snapped up by property developers before we could get a look in or raise enough funds for the purchase or rental.

Thus, there was setback after setback and it was a difficult time to fundraise, as most statutory bodies were revising their funding strategies and moving away from grant-aid, towards commissioning, as well as abandoning their support for innovatory work. Without a track record at that time, it was difficult to make a case for the Bethel vision, though we were successful in raising some funds. One grant enabled us to take on a couple of consultants to develop Bethel; they provided basic support in developing policies and staff contracts but did not support our vision of finding a building or site to develop the vision of a healing and healthy living centre. This was a period of reversal – see Chapter 7.

Despite all these frustrations, other things were beginning to come together, the first of which was the doula project, which initially came out of the parish nursing initiative.

Chapter 4 – The Development of the Doula Project

A doula is defined as a non-medical companion who provides support to a mother during pregnancy, childbirth, and after the birth. There is considerable evidence to demonstrate that women who are supported by a doula during labour and childbirth are less likely to require a Caesarean birth or to need pain relief, and they are more likely to give birth spontaneously, have a shorter labour, and feel satisfied with their birthing experience. Research also shows that women who have a doula throughout the prenatal period and childbirth are less likely to have a preterm delivery or a low birthweight baby, less likely to experience postpartum depression, and more likely to initiate and continue breastfeeding for a longer period.

It was the parish nursing that initially led us down the doula route. In the course of her community work in Sparkbrook, Mary, the parish nurse, came across a housing association property which housed female asylum seekers, some of them pregnant. So, Mary started developing various activities in the community for these women and others living nearby: health advice and health checks, gardening, visits to a spa, picnics, barbecues, a Fit4Life group for the elderly, trips away for people with long-term illness. She was joined for a period by a second parish nurse, Liz, who was a member of Christ Church and they recruited a team of volunteers.

One of the first women that Mary supported was E, who had fled for her life, after being attacked by a gang in her home country, Zimbabwe. She had come to the UK via Zambia and South Africa. E gave birth to a baby girl who was born with a very serious heart condition and the baby had to have several operations at the children's hospital, before being discharged on long-term medication. Mary called on her team of volunteers to visit E at the hospital, to support her and to pray for E and the baby. E was so grateful for this that she told other women she knew about the support she had received from Bethel. And so, the volunteer team grew and was used to support other isolated women who were pregnant and they became Bethel's first team of volunteer doulas. Another qualified social worker, Abi, also joined the volunteer team at this time, giving another perspective to the work, together with Mary and Liz.

During the 2009-10 financial year, 28 women received Bethel doula support, with a further 17 who were pregnant, awaiting childbirth; they were from 14 different nationalities (Chinese, Zimbabwean, Somalian, Eritrean, White English, Pakistani, Ugandan, Nigerian, Ethiopian, Congolese, Jamaican, Polish, Romanian and other Asian). Many of the volunteer doulas gave as much as 10 hours per week of support and some of them had previously been beneficiaries of the project. All of them received training, from a health visitor and a qualified doula and midwife.

Statistics show that Birmingham has a particularly high level of perinatal mortality (the death of a baby around the time of the birth) and I was convinced that Bethel's doula work ought therefore to attract NHS funding. This did ultimately happen but not for another 5-6 years. In the meantime, we were able to attract three-year funding from Comic Relief. This funding enabled us to employ a part-time manager for the doula project and Debbie worked for Bethel in this capacity for three years. We had to provide Comic Relief with regular monitoring statistics and case studies, and after the 3 years, we were able to use this information to prepare an evaluation report of the work, to send to potential funders to enable it to continue. It gave us the track record we needed to attract substantial funding, as Comic Relief had required Bethel to give Doula support to at least 30 women a year and this target was easily achieved and surpassed.

Further funding came to the project during this period from the People's Health Trust and the Social Enterprise Investment Fund, as well as a grant for the doula work from Sandwell and West Birmingham Primary Care Trust and then later from Clinical Commissioning Groups (CCGs) in Birmingham, Solihull and Sandwell. The William Cadbury Trust also supported the doula work but two successive lottery bids, to fund the whole Bethel vision, were not successful.

One of the things Comic Relief had requested was a feedback report from the women who were helped by the doula project. Mary had organised one of her picnics and I used this opportunity to talk to the women who attended the picnic with their babies/children, asking them how the project had helped them. Some of them did not speak English but, through translators, I was still able to find out that all of them, without exception, were extremely grateful for the doula support. They also appreciated opportunities, like this picnic, to meet other women (peers) who were in a similar situation to themselves. As a result of these findings, we established a mother and toddler group for these women and their babies, which still continues to this day. Initially, this was set up in conjunction with another Christian project that came out of the same prophecy, Stepping Stones, who already worked with families and children. Later, when Stepping Stones lost their funding and closed, the mother and baby group was taken under the Bethel umbrella.

Mothers and their babies and toddlers gathering for a Doula picnic at Cannon Hill Park

At the Doula Picnic

At a Doula picnic

Once NHS funding had been obtained, Bethel was able to build further on its doula work, to recruit more staff and to expand the work, so that the target numbers of isolated, at-risk mothers were substantially increased. Margaret became Doula Manager in 2014 and we later employed three paid senior doulas, a volunteer manager and administrative staff. A team of 30 volunteers were also recruited and trained to be volunteer doulas. The funding continued, despite the NHS going through two re-organisations, from PCTs to CCGs, and more recently to Integrated Care Organisations but this full development of the work came much later. Several other things had to happen first.

People being supported through the Doula Project received help to attend antenatal appointments, to register with a GP (if they did not have one), doulas visited them at the places where they were accommodated (many of them in unfriendly hostel accommodation or B&B hotels). Each woman also received a Moses basket full of items needed for a newborn baby, nappies, baby clothing, bottles, blankets etc and a doula also stayed with them during labour and the birth of the baby, if they wanted this. Once the baby was born, there was further support in learning how to care for the baby, with parenting classes, if needed, and help with breast-feeding. Referral for mental health support, if needed (eg post-natal depression or other trauma-related problems they had). And all were encouraged to attend the mother and baby group. Referrals were received from midwives, social workers, the NHS, other groups working with asylum seekers (eg Red Cross, Restore etc), health visitors and by self-referral.

Chapter 5 – E's story

In the previous chapter, I have talked about E, who was the first mother that Bethel gave doula support to. But E's subsequent story has shown how much her life's journey has inter-twined with the visions and pictures given to Bethel in its early stages. So, I am going to devote a whole chapter to this amazing African woman and her story, who originally came to the UK as an asylum seeker.

E first came to Bethel's attention, through Mary, the parish nurse. She had given birth to a baby girl who was born with a severe heart abnormality. The baby needed urgent open-heart surgery twice during her first weeks of life and was in intensive care at the Children's Hospital. Mary got together a group of volunteers to pray with E and for the baby. It was the start of the Doula project.

One of the volunteers who supported E was May, from my church, as well as Abi from a social work background. After the initial traumas associated with the surgery, the baby was discharged home on special medication. May invited E and her partner to attend my church. Then to join the worship group, where it turned out that E had a wonderful singing voice, as well as leadership potential. Several years later, she became a talented worship leader and a deacon of the church, a woman filled and led by the power of the Holy Spirit.

I am telling her story because I believe that she is the embodiment of the pictures and visions that were given during prayer in the early months of Bethel. Many of the women helped through the Doula Project are asylum seekers, like E, who have escaped from their countries of birth and so have very little contact with their families. Some of them had to flee for their lives from their home country. And we all know that the UK doesn't exactly welcome asylum seekers. If pregnant, they are further isolated from those who might give them support around the time of the birth of their babies – their families and friends. I think that their situations are like the picture we were given of people trapped in mud. And the people leaning over and pulling them out of the mud and sprinkling them with clean water are Bethel's Doula Team.

E was no exception and she was in particular distress about the health of her baby daughter. After she was invited to join my church, she also received the anointing of the Holy Spirit. Thus, she was one of those who came to drink from the chalice of pure living water. Her testimony is very powerful and leads others to Christ. Sadly, she lost her daughter just before her 3rd birthday and this was absolutely devastating for E. People from my church gave her the support she needed, as well as the doula team. And God has blessed her since with 3 sons and now a daughter. E was later awarded British citizenship (she had to take several exams to receive this, one of which was a test of her ability to speak and write good English). This year, she took a GCSE exam in English and is currently awaiting the result. Her sons are doing well in British schools and very much involved in church life and Sunday school activities. Both E and her partner, whom she married, have been baptised at my church by full immersion.

Many others who have been helped by the Doula Project could give similar testimonies. Some of their stories are included later in Chapter 8.

Before I move on, I want to talk about the doula work and how I have come to realise that I had a doula myself, without realising it, when I gave birth to my son. I had fled almost 2,000 miles across Australia, from domestic violence, and had ended up homeless, starving and pregnant on the streets of Sydney. During my journey south, I made contact with a friend and she sent a midwife friend of hers, who lived in Sydney, to contact me. Margaret was a great support and helped me to find somewhere to live, and through the latter stages of pregnancy, labour and in the neonatal period. She also kept in touch when I returned to England eight months later, by remembering my son, Ben, on each of his birthdays. So, I can testify to the importance of a doula in your life, especially if you are isolated, homeless and without family support. Both E and

I, and others who have been helped by Bethel, were pretty broken and shattered, when first put in touch with a doula. And the doula helped to put together the shattered pieces of our lives.

Chapter 6 – Other healthy living activities

A People's Health Trust grant enabled Bethel to branch into new areas of health work. But the grant was for only one year (2011-2012) and it was given for health promotion in the local community; we used it to create two part-time posts, who were based in Small Heath at my church. Laura and Ester were appointed and set up some successful healthy living activities in the area - a Walk for Wellbeing and Bhangra Dancing sessions (below).

These activities gained a good following and some momentum but, sadly no further funding was forthcoming when the funding ran out, so had to be discontinued.

But it was later possible to establish a second arm of Bethel's services in 2018, which was called the Rapha Project. This is fully described in Chapter 8.

Much later in the project, the staff have developed follow-on activities for clients who have been helped by both arms of Bethel; these have included:

Creative workshops (such as jewellery making and other crafts); a peer-support group for mothers who have lost a baby or child and information sessions on health-related issues.

Chapter 7 – Reversals

In Volume I of "The Desert Will Rejoice," I described the concept of *Reversals (*page 44 in volume I). These are periods in the development of Christian work when everything seems to go wrong from a human perspective, despite huge efforts on the part of the Christians trying to develop the vision. Others have suggested that we look at these periods from God's point of view, rather than from our own. And I quote directly from Chapter 2 in this first volume:

"You would think that, if God loves us so much..., he would lead us not into troublesome situations but away from them....At such times we cry out: Why is God allowing this to happen to me? How can God say he loves me when he fails to answer my prayers and deliver me from such dark and difficult situations .... It might appear at the surface of things that the Almighty has lost control – but nothing could be further from the truth. God never loses control of anything. If you could penetrate the depths of the divine heart, you would see purpose being worked out that would more than compensate for your feelings of uncertainty and doubt..."

These words are taken from some Bible reading notes "Everyday with Jesus", written in

1987 by Selwyn Hughes and published by CWA. He goes on to say:

"It is now time to ask the question: why does God adopt these strange and mysterious methods of working? He does it, not because he wants to tantalise us, or play games, but because there is just no other way he can bring about his perfect purposes.

"You see, when God reveals something to us, he knows that, at the moment of some fresh unfolding of his will, we will have within us a combination of Godly concerns and human perspectives. We are eager, alert and full of natural enthusiasm. He knows that our natural enthusiasm is the thing that helps us to get going to do his bidding, but a moment has to come when our natural enthusiasm is overlaid by divine perspectives.

"How does God achieve this? He allows us to go ahead in the strength of our own eagerness and then, at the appropriate moment, he changes gear and puts things into reverse. When we come to this point we realise that, if the revelation that God has given us is to be realised, it will not be because of our strength and prowess – but his.

"When we learn that lesson, then God miraculously intervenes to restore his purposes. Note the word 'miraculously.' The fact that things are restored 'miraculously' is then a constant reminder that God must always have the biggest part in a project. In that way, *no onlooker can be in doubt as to who is responsible – everyone recognises it to be God."*

A big time of reversal for the Bethel Health and Healing Project came in 2010-2012, four years after we had registered the project as a charity and company limited by guarantee. We had just come to the end of some 3-year funding from Comic Relief for the Doula Project and this funding was not going to be continued. By this time, the doula work was well established and had been helping isolated pregnant women for several years. We also had an embryonic counselling service under the Bethel umbrella, led by a board member, Pauline.

But during a period of several years there were many struggles for the Bethel Health and Healing Network. Many ups and downs, including the loss of the base where we had planned to develop the Bethel vision. In about 2010, several people on Bethel's Board and other staff and volunteers started to resign and drift away from Bethel and I became very isolated and depressed in trying to take the full vision forward. I felt discouraged and as if I had lost my way. I began to think that maybe I had got everything wrong. *"Did God really speak to me about this?"* Were the stunning pictures I had received, just a result of an overactive imagination? Or wishful thinking? Why had God chosen me to bring about the Bethel vision? I was not anything special and indeed had areas of wounding in my own life, which might preclude me from being strong for others.

During this period I went on a silent retreat to check that God still wanted me to take it forward. During the retreat God constantly affirmed that the vision for Bethel was of him and was not out of my own imagination. He particularly affirmed the concept of "Living Water" and, towards the end of the retreat, urged me to put into writing the details of the vision for Bethel, as so many people had come on board over the last few years, bringing their own visions. So, we had got distracted. In the process of writing this vision on paper, God led me to consider and include all of those things that had helped me during my own life, supports that had enabled me to rebuild my life after it had been shattered when I was just 19 years old.

A particular division had come about the parish nursing work, which some did not feel was in keeping with the original vision for Bethel. At an awayday, the nurses were challenged about this, in a critical way that made me wince. Not long after that the two parish nurses pulled out from under the Bethel umbrella, though the doula work continued. This was a huge loss to Bethel – losing the parish nurses. I do hope parish nurses come back on board at some time in the future, as part of working out the Bethel vision.

For me, the vision of the Bethel Project has always been about a place, a friendly place, a building where all the activities would be based.

In the early years, it was difficult to fund our own building and I also found lots of opposition to the concept of having our own building, as much of the Doula work operated out in the community. People were very strongly identifying with the Doula work and some felt that this would be endangered if we were to develop new strands of health work, or seek funds to obtain a building, which might then become a financial burden.

I consider this issue to be a reversal – or maybe the impact of spiritual warfare - the setting up of a "Bethel Centre" – a building where all the vision would be developed and carried out. It was to be a welcoming place, easy to access on a bus route, where support for people in need, and various therapies and healthy-living activities would be based, as well as counselling and listening sessions. All of these activities would help people to get their lives back together.

Bethel had been set up from scratch, so had no financial resources of its own to acquire and/or refurbish a building. Those who know Birmingham will realise that there are lots of empty buildings in the city, especially in the inner city. Yet, try as we did, none of the buildings we identified as suitable, were acquired. In the last 20 years, we have probably looked at 20 or more buildings, most of which were owned by other organisations or people. Yet, one by one, they slipped through our fingers. Indeed, there were four or more that were actually *stolen* from us by people with other agendas. And, here in 2024, we are still without our own building, though renting space from the Jericho Foundation (a fellow prophecy project). But, as I write, two of the Bethel trustees have managed to get additional space for Bethel, through NHS contacts, a whole floor over a GP practice. So, this has been a reversal of 20 years or more. We continue to pray that God will provide the right place for Bethel to base its activities and that it is affordable and suitable to develop the full vision.

We had also received a substantial grant from a government agency to do some work developing Bethel as a social enterprise. We took on a consultant agency to do this work for us. They were not Christians and they didn't catch the full vision either, refused to search for a building for the Bethel work, and then wrote their final report as a major critique of everything that Bethel was doing. It was a very low point for the Bethel vision.

In 2012, I had to go into hospital for a major operation and, while I was recovering, but still out of action, some of these divisions between the Board and the volunteers and staff began to grow. It would seem as if everybody saw the vision for Bethel and its work in a different way and each had different plans for how best to take it forward. People started to get offended by each other and then resigned. So, we lost crucial volunteers and staff and most of the Board, including the chairman. At that time, I was still in a weak, post-operative state. I wanted to resign myself, to stop all the pain and accompanying accusations that were being directed at me too, but I couldn't do that. I couldn't give up. I couldn't let the Lord down. The only thing that kept me going was the visions the Lord had given me at the start, especially the chalice of living water that the Lord had placed in my hands, as well as his call to obedience.

   Three months after I came out of hospital, I had a letter from my good friend, Janet, who had helped in the development of Jericho. She knew I was struggling and these were the words she wrote in her letter to me:

Hi Christine,

Here is the message I believe God gave me about Bethel. I have tried not to alter what I believe he said to me. It seems to me that there was almost a *tetchy* air about it! As if God was saying "I've told you this before".

1. Bottom line: "Do you believe that I asked for <u>three</u> projects? If so, Bethel is very important.
2. Consider who remains loyal to the original vision of Bethel and discern together my will and purpose for it. Be very certain of my heart and mind.
3. Cut away the *deadwood* – all those who would stir up and muddle my vision.
4. "Christine, I will give you all the strength you need <u>as</u> you need it."
5. "Accept there may still be a long haul before Bethel is up and running…. but.."
6. "You have my assurance that Bethel <u>will be</u> established in my time and for my purpose."

Janet.

This encouraging message from Janet had the effect of giving me the perseverance I needed to keep going. Another encouragement came from my Pastor at that time, Dave Ellis, who was praying with me about Bethel. He shared with me that he felt the Lord had revealed to him that Bethel was going to be huge. At that time, it felt to me like it was collapsing and that it wouldn't survive, let alone be *huge*. How wrong I was!

What had happened to the Bethel vision during this low period reminds me of the Biblical story of Gideon in *Judges 6*. An Angel of the Lord appeared to him, saying *"Mighty Warrior, The Lord is with you."* But Gideon questioned how the Lord could be with them after all that had happened to them. He also questioned his own ability as he was from the lowliest clan and the youngest in his family. But Gideon was given a task by the Lord and was sent to do it, with the words *"Go in the strength that you have…..Am I not sending you?"*

During the low period of 2010-12, two amazing things actually happened, which brought Bethel out of that particular reversal:

1. Bethel was granted full funding of its Doula Project by an NHS body, the local Clinical Commissioning Group (see Chapter 4).
2. An outgoing Board member, introduced me to a friend of hers, whom she thought

would make an ideal new Chair for the Bethel charity.

That person was Jacynth Ivey, who first became a trustee of the charity and then went onto chair the Board for ten years. The next chapters describe some of the developments that Jacynth's leadership, and the extra funding, brought to the Bethel Health and Healing Network.

There was another reversal, about 9-10 years later, about the time of the Covid-19 pandemic, when we also lost several key people to the project, both staff and trustees, and it was followed with a sustained period of severe financial constraint but I will describe this in the next chapter.

Jacynth Ivey

<u>Chapter 8</u> – The Growth of Bethel

When Jacynth became chair of Bethel, she got to work straight away and first encouraged us to take on a part-time CEO/fundraiser. I knew what little money we had in the bank to do this but, amazingly, it worked out well and it took a lot of the weight off my shoulders. Jeanette started with Bethel as a part-time CEO in 2014 for 2-3 years, then left for a while, but is currently a trustee on the Bethel Board. Since Jeanette, we have had three more CEOs: Georgina, Madge and currently Jennifer. Each has played a different part in developing the Bethel Project and its vision. Georgina moved Bethel's base from Sparkbrook to Balsall Heath in 2017, a next-door ward of the inner city, and gave great support to the Doula project. Madge organised two fund-raising balls and established some significant partnerships. Jennifer began in 2022 and brought to Bethel some significant business and development skills, as well as strengthening and building on Bethel's partnership with the Living Well Consortium and NHS bodies.

    Shortly after the end of the first reversal, Margaret was appointed as Doula Manager and she is still with Bethel. Margaret is an experienced midwife and NHS manager. We also took on a Volunteer Manager about the same time, to recruit and enable the training of a team of volunteers. Currently in this post is Calis. All these first staff posts were part-time and they remain so.

Jacynth also implemented two envisioning sessions during her first months as chair, leading to the production of a more business-like approach in the charity, as well as a set of values for the organisation. In 2017, she guided the charity into producing its first Strategic Plan and this, in turn, sharpened Bethel's focus, leading firstly to the taking on of a staff member to develop other health-related activities, as well as expanding the staff team to strengthen the Doula Project. New trustees also joined the Board.

We had taken on a consultant, Santosh, in 2017, to help develop and write the first strategic plan. This document had a momentous effect on Bethel's subsequent development, as it contained an analysis of community needs, as well as encompassing the whole vision. And Santosh has continued to work in several different roles for Bethel, in the years since then, as a consultant, then a staff member and is currently the Operations Manager.

Drawing on the community analyses in the strategic plan, I submitted a bid to the Tudor Trust, which was successful and provided Bethel with 3-years' funding towards a new post, the role of which was to develop new streams of health-related work. We decided to call this new arm of the work, the Rapha Project. We also took on a new board member, Mei, who was a Clinical

Psychologist, and she encouraged the Rapha Project to focus on developing a Reflective Listening Service, rather than continuing the counselling, as there were other bodies in the city who offered counselling. This listening service became very popular.

During this period (2017-2020), the Bethel Project established a base at the premises of the Jericho project, in Balsall Heath, and also started working with Interserve, who were developing a new centre, St John's House, in Alum Rock. The Rapha Project was initially based at St. John's House, through partnerships with Acorn Christian Healing Foundation, who provided training in reflective listening techniques, and Interserve, who purchased and refitted the building. Volunteers were recruited to undertake this training to become "Listeners." The Listening Service soon became over-subscribed, so that the Rapha Manager had to establish a waiting list.

    A number of different people have led in the development of the Rapha Project.

    Following the Tudor Trust grant, most of the development activity focused on raising awareness, recruiting volunteers and building partnerships to start linking into local health and wellbeing pathways. Based at St Johns, Alum Rock, another deprived inner city area, this picked up momentum under Kelly Cranston, who visited and connected with all manner of organisations such as local GPs, community centres, local neighbourhood offices, other charities etc.

The first service users received support in October 2018, with 12 service users being supported in the first five months. A drop-in coffee morning 'Tea, Cake and Me', run by volunteers at St Johns was also set up for service users and local people. Service delivery was slow at first but started to show an upward trend; 30 people were engaged in 2019/20, with the support of 11 volunteers. By April 2020, 116 people had been supported. All listening sessions were face to face at this stage. One of the volunteers, Sue, began to build relationships with social prescribers and reviewed Bethel's IT structures; she also hosted "Permission to Smile," a mental health initiative for service users of both arms of Bethel (Doula and Rapha); this was funded by Greggs.

In March 2020, Covid-19 hit and Bethel went into lockdown, when referrals dried up and volunteers left. A new approach was needed and protocols were developed for a telephone listening service. This became very popular, though some individuals who had been receiving face to face support did not want to transition to the telephone service. A small number were waiting for face-to-face to resume. The outcome was that both face-to-face and telephone listening services were eventually offered and this resulted in an upsurge in the number of people requesting listening support. During 2021-2022, 172 service users were supported through the listening sessions.

Bethel was able to secure additional funding to enable them to continue functioning during and after the lockdown. This came from the Neighbourhood Networks Schemes and the Eveson Trust. There was quite a turnover of staff during this period, with Kathy (previously a Senior Doula) and Lindsay helping for short periods as well as two consultants (Rosie and Santosh).

Post-lockdown, there was an upsurge in requests for listening support, as many people had been struggling with the isolation imposed during the pandemic lockdown period but at present the service is functioning well, though short of all the funding that is needed. The current manager for this work is Alison, with the help of two assistants and a team of volunteers.

The Doula Project was always over-subscribed as well, with more people being referred for support than funding that was available. The client groups for this project are isolated pregnant women, many of them asylum seekers, but also teenage mothers and other women without support. The initial PCT funding was carried over into the CCGs and beyond. The NHS bodies seem very happy with the work that Bethel is doing with this needy client group. The Mother & Toddler Group, established back in 2012, still continues and is very much valued by the mothers who have come through the Doula Project, as it provides friendships and peer support from other mothers with a similar background.

The lockdown affected many voluntary organisations and some did not survive it. Many, along with Bethel, have had to continue with severe financial restrictions. As a result of the pandemic, the NHS was under severe financial strain too, and Bethel's doula work is mostly NHS funded, so Bethel was affected financially as well. Last year, Bethel's Board had to put together a contingency strategy, in case promised NHS funding was not realised. Amazingly, at the 11th hour, a large chunk of delayed NHS funding came through, so the contingency plan was not needed. It had been another time of reversal. But from my perspective, I could not believe that God, who spoke so clearly about the need for the establishment of Bethel, would not continue to provide the resources needed for it.

At the AGM in October 2023, an Impact Report was released, which showed how most of the service users of both projects were thoroughly satisfied with the service they had received. Some described it as life-changing. This report can be found on the Bethel website: https://www.bethelnetwork.org.uk. The statistics in the report showed that, during 2022-23, for the Doula Project 321 referrals were received, 282 women supported, 254 home visits made and 1116 support sessions delivered by the Doula service. The Rapha project supported 131 people, through 484 sessions and provided 383 hours of support, with 94% of people being satisfied with the service. The original report also includes case studies of clients accessing both of Bethel's services, as well as some of the volunteers. Costings included in the Impact Report show how much money the UK's statutory services have been saved because of the services provided by Bethel Health and Healing Network.

Five of the current Bethel staff team: Santosh (Operations Manager), Alison (Rapha Manager), Jennifer (CEO), Calis (Volunteer Manager) and Margaret (Doula Manager)

Bethel Health and Healing Network has also won several awards:
BVSC Volunteer Team of the Year, 2017
Bex Live Health and Well-being Promotion, 2018
Chairs award Sandwell & West Birmingham CCG
Equality Award 2018
Thrive awards 2018

The Bethel Centre has still not been fully established but two board members, Jon Hindle and Duncan Moore (now Chair), together with CEO Jennifer, are taking this forward, and Bethel has just moved into a new location in Nechells where it has a suite of offices, free-of-charge at an NHS building, in close proximity to local GPs.

This provides accommodation for both arms of Bethel, as well as developing other services for the women who use the Doula Project.

2023 IMPACT REPORT

Bethel Doula provides emotional, practical and birth partner support to vulnerable and isolated pregnant women and new mothers. We work with statutory and community partners across the health and social care sectors to ensure that vulnerable women and their children do not fall between the gaps in services. We supplement our face-to-face support with on-line activities, mother and baby group support, parenting skills courses and connect mothers and families to other support services. In 2023, 321 referrals were received, 254 home visits were made, 1116 support sessions delivered and 282 women supported. 84% said they would recommend the service, 89% were satisfied with the service.

Bethel Rapha provides a safe, non-judgmental listening service to adults experiencing anxiety, stress, isolation and depression often caused by the wider determinants of health such as social and economic conditions, difficult family and personal relationships, racism and sexism and other discrimination. In addition to telephone support, we work in partnership with statutory and community organisations to deliver face to face listening sessions in community settings across Birmingham and Solihull. People accessing the service receive up to 9 hours of listening support and signposting to additional mental health and wellbeing services. In 2023, 131 people were supported through 484 sessions, with 383 hours of support being provided. 92% said they would recommend the service, 94% were satisfied with the service, 64% said their mental health was improved.

CASE STUDIES FROM THE IMPACT REPORT

E's story in Chapter 5 has been complemented by so many others as hundreds of women have now been helped by the Doula Project. Here are just a few:

Doula case study 1

F was referred to Bethel Doula Service by her midwife, after she observed that she had no support network in Birmingham, having recently moved from London. F had undergone a traumatic birth with her first child three years earlier, followed by a miscarriage. Not long after the miscarriage, she discovered she was pregnant again. F was matched with a senior doula, who attended hospital appointments with her and helped her to arrange a debrief at the hospital regarding the traumatic birth of her first child, and the subsequent advice and management of the miscarriage.

The senior doula provided F with emotional support throughout the pregnancy and helped her make informed decisions regarding the birth plan and prepare for her choice to have a scheduled Caesarean section. F stated, *"Following my first child, I led a very isolated life, leading me to suffer from postnatal depression. I am certain that, had I been referred to Bethel during this time, I would have had a better pre-and post-birth experience, which I got after the birth of my second child."*

F again suffered from post-natal depression, and the senior doula attended several post-birth hospital appointments with her. She helped her understand that what she was experiencing was common and that she need not suffer in silence as she had the first time. With the help of the senior doula, medication and therapy, F fully recovered and was able to be the best mother to her children.

F stated that the Doula Service enabled her to engage with an experienced person who helped her understand her issues, choices available, and better plan for the pending birth, thereby reducing anxiety. She was also better able to manage her mental health, and therefore her toddler and new baby, with less fear and anxiety. F commented, *"I did not require the attendance of other health professionals such as the mental health team, or a longer stay in hospital - maternity or mental health. I was not separated from my toddler or baby to have my mental health managed."*

F is now volunteering and preparing to start a career as a midwife in 2024.

Doula Case Study 2
T came to the UK as a postgraduate student with her husband and son, and soon after found that she was pregnant with triplets. T was referred to the Doula Service post-birth. Following heavy bleeding and the premature birth of the triplets one of the babies died soon after delivery. T stated that she did not have time to grieve. *"That period was a difficult moment for us in my family,*

as we were settling in the country, and did not understand the system." The bereavement team supported her with the funeral arrangements as she did not have recourse to public funds.

T stated her mental health and that of her husband had been affected and there were times when she felt "emotionally numbed, suicidal, and generally tired." One weekend when at her lowest, she contemplated suicide as she'd had a tough week – the newborns had attended different hospitals on more than one occasion that week – treated for chest infections, including short inpatient stays. T's husband had sourced, organised, and paid the first month's rent for a flat they were promised. They had saved money from limited funds for the removal van and packed up their belongings including baby clothes and food and transferred them to what was to be their new accommodation. They were pleased to be moving away from the cold house and the dark creeping mould which repeatedly returned even after they cleaned it. Whilst preparing to finally leave the old accommodation, T and husband were informed that the new property was no longer available. They were distraught as all their belongings had been removed and left outside in heavy rain. This included food, which could not be salvaged. Following referral to the Doula Service, T and her family received emotional support, resources for the babies, food parcels, and a referral to Early Help services. She was signposted to an organisation where she received a debriefing for baby loss. The suicidal thoughts became less invasive, and her self-esteem and ability to cope with everyday challenges improved. T stated that she appreciated the Doula Service for being an *'amicable organisation when they needed help.'*

Rapha Listening Service Case Study 1
S, a middle-aged Pakistani woman, self-referred to the Rapha Listening Service with a long history of anxiety and depression. At the initial assessment, she spoke of her ongoing challenges with her mental health, which was now being exacerbated by concerns about finances and her ability to provide for her dependents.

S attended nine listening sessions with her trained listener and used the time to discuss her fears of having 'another nervous breakdown,' panic attacks, the needs of her family, and the rising cost of living. She was also supported to contact her Community Mental Health Team and a pending appointment was brought forward, resulting in an increase in medication, which helped stabilise her mental health, preventing further deterioration. She also accepted a referral for an assessment of her social needs and was offered and accepted help from family support services. While S was often tearful during her listening sessions, she always expressed gratitude that someone had listened to her whilst she tried to deal with the complexities of her personal issues. At the final evaluation, S was positive about the support she had received and commented that her listener had really helped with appropriate signposting. S was also able to 'get things off her chest' and was now more hopeful that 'things might change'.

<u>Rapha Listening Service Case Study 2</u>
A, an Indian woman in her mid-30s, was referred to the Listening Service by her GP with a history of anxiety, depression, and insomnia due to poor physical health. On initial assessment, she spoke of a history of suicidal thoughts and what triggered them. A was matched with a listener, and she used the 9 weekly sessions to discuss relationship issues, negotiation skills, adopting a positive mindset and managing anxiety and worries. During the sessions, a new work issue arose whereby A felt she was being unfairly treated by others.

The focus now changed to building strength, resilience and self–advocacy. A identified that although things were difficult, she was 'keeping on going and staying positively minded'. As the sessions progressed, she became more confident about her plans to address the work issues. While suicidal thoughts had been an important disclosure for A during her initial assessment, she no longer raised this issue during the listening sessions as she became more confident. At the end of the support evaluation, A said that the listener's kindness and support had boosted her mood and that she had looked forward to the sessions. Overall, she felt that the sessions helped her cope with her difficulties and that she was now in a 'much better place.'

Rapha Listening Service Case Study 3
Quote from a white British male, 75, history of relationships issues.
"I really appreciate the listening services and my listener, as I felt these sessions improved my self-confidence and motivation."

So, this has described the growth of Bethel to where it is today. Of necessity, I have crammed more than 10 years' development into a few chapters but I hope it demonstrates the journey that Bethel has been on and how staff dedication has brought it to where it is today. I have tried to keep some cohesion to the story but this has meant that not all the story is chronological – I have jumped about in time. There is still much planned but I believe that the organisation is well on its way to reaching the vision which started it all off.

Jennifer, the current CEO of Bethel has many plans for future development and has summarised these in a wall chart in her office which has a large central message of **THINK BIG,** surrounded by 14 smaller boxes listing areas for expansion or developing new work. Some of these are about developing new income streams to enable the Bethel work to become sustainable. Areas for expansion included:

Men's health, bereavement support, menopause support, expansion into neighbouring areas, working with others to provide housing for those in need, developing training programmes in becoming a doula or a listener, social activities. So, Bethel Health and Healing Network is still a small charity but has a big vision. This puts me in the mind of the comments made 12 years ago by Pastor Dave: Bethel is going to be HUGE! (see Chapter 7).

So, Bethel is now grounded and on its way. It has a highly committed and experienced staff team and the work is rooted in prayer. Some of the vision described in earlier chapters has not yet been developed but I believe that, in time, and with this team, these will be added to Bethel's mission activities.

THINK BIG

A Poem about Bethel, composed by a staff member

BETHEL

When the doors of Bethel opened,
The treasures within shone,
Like beacons of hope
On the dull landscape,
Where some blossomed and thrived,
While others merely survived.

And for those in the shadows
fighting for survival
Came a season of change,
With Christine's arrival.

Arms were stretched out wide, embracing
The last, the least, the lonesome.
Bethel shone like a star
A real Place of Welcome

Pregnant she came,
Thinking nobody cared.
Wrapped in love
Her birth was now shared

Depressed he came,
So sad and alone,
He now had a listener
For chats on the phone.

Afraid she came
admitting defeat,
empowered and affirmed
now stood on her feet.

Lonely he came
From far, far away….
He found community,
Strength for each day.

The doors of Bethel are now open,
the treasures within shine,
like beacons of hope
on the dull landscape.

Alison Thompson 2023

Chapter 9 – The Cairn Consortium

Back in 2012, when I was still recovering from my operation, I had a phone call from the Deputy CEO of the Jericho Foundation, Carlo, one of the founder members of staff of Jericho. He told me he had had a dream and would like to discuss it with me. So we met and prayed together. Carlo was very much aware of the three projects arising from the prophecy given to Maria Blom in 1986. He felt that the three projects should work together more closely, each retaining its individual charitable status but maybe coming under an umbrella body to provide cohesion and stability to them. He thought they might also share some back-office functions.

As a result of this, Jeanette and Jacynth facilitated some meetings of senior members of staff and boards of each of the three organisations – Gilgal, Jericho and Bethel. It was decided to set up a consortium, and they met regularly to share and to pray together. The consortium was later given a name "Cairn" from the story in Joshua 4: 4-9, after the crossing of the River Jordan. This was to commemorate another miracle: the River Jordan was in flood but God parted the waters of the river, so that the whole nation of Israel could cross over on the river bed. A leader from each tribe was asked to pick up a stone from the bed of the river and to carry it over to the other side, to make a pile of 12 stones – or a **cairn.** In Joshua 4: 20-24, reads:

"And Joshua set up at Gilgal the twelve stones they had taken out of the Jordan. He said to the Israelites, "In the future when your descendants asked their fathers, "What do these stones mean?" tell them 'Israel crossed the Jordan on dry ground' For the Lord your God dried up the Jordan before you until you had crossed over. The Lord your God did what he had done to the Red Sea, when he dried it up before us until we had crossed over. He did this so that the peoples of the earth might know that the hand of the Lord is powerful and so that you might always fear the Lord your God."

I believe that Cairn is an appropriate name for the consortium for God's hand had been so obvious in the setting up and continuation of these projects: Gilgal, Jericho and Bethel. There have been miraculous signs, divine coincidences, unexpected provision and divine inspiration in the setting up of these amazing projects, all of them working with client groups who have been in severe difficulties.

And now, as I write this in 2024, I can report that the consortium is in the process of setting up a new joint project, in the building that had first been provided for the setting up of Gilgal. "That's the Place!" The new joint project is to be called 'Live, Work, Heal,' as each of the three projects will be working together in providing for new client groups through collaboration and co-operation.

Volume I of "The Desert Will Rejoice" started with the envisioning and development of Gilgal, and described the development of Jericho. Now Volume II of "The Desert Will Rejoice" mainly describes the third part of the prophecy, Bethel, which had only just begun when Volume I was published in 2004.

End Piece

So, this book has described the development of the vision of the Bethel Health and Healing Network during the period 2004 to 2024. To bring visions into reality requires a whole raft of people, with different skills and abilities and motivations, to work together. So many people have come on board at different times to help bring this about. I want to acknowledge in this End Piece all of these people, some of whom have been named in this book and others not, but every single one of them has played their part in bringing the vision to reality. I want to make it clear that this hasn't just been up to me, despite Alison mentioning me in her poem, printed elsewhere. I included the poem to demonstrate how much all the staff and volunteers just love working for the Bethel Health and Healing Network and some want to show their appreciation through poetry.

   I also want to acknowledge all of those people who have played a part in the writing, illustration and publishing of this book. In particular, Santosh Rai (details of the Rapha work); Jennifer Jones-Rigby (future plans for the Bethel Network); Sabrina Nolan Jacques (artwork for the front cover and one of the illustrations in chapter 1); Brian Opiyo, a Ugandan artist (two pieces of artwork); Ken Hazel (commenting on the manuscript); and Duncan Moore (for writing the Foreword). I am so grateful to all of them for supporting this publication.

In the early chapters of this book, I have talked about the visions and revelations that God brought, to motivate me to work with others to establish Bethel Health and Healing Network. And the later chapters include the practical details of establishing the project which, to some, may seem to be a mile away from the original words and visions. I leave the readers to judge this for themselves.

When Janet Harmer sent me her words of encouragement in 2012 (see chapter 7), we could not have seen 12 years into the future to what Bethel is today. I am so glad that she encouraged me to keep going, as the project has helped so many different people, some to come to faith and others just to keep going in very depriving and traumatizing circumstances. And David, Janet's husband, who sadly passed away last year, gave us this wonderful passion flower image which remains as the Bethel logo, an embodiment of everything that Bethel has become. God's word has definitely not returned to him void (Isaiah 55: 11 (NIV)):

"So is my word that goes out from my mouth: It will not return to me empty, but will accomplish what I desire and achieve the purpose for which I sent it."

I started in the introduction to this book by giving a brief testimony of my life. The decision to do this came to me whilst writing the story of Bethel because I believe that my own life story is so bound up in Bethel's journey and what it is now doing, though I couldn't have predicted this in advance. Perhaps I can illustrate this best by drawing on a sermon that my current pastor, Owen, gave recently.

He described the Japanese art of *Kintsugi*, which restores broken pottery into something that is beautiful and valuable. When a piece of pottery shatters into many pieces, it is tempting to throw it away. But the Japanese collect all the pieces and join them together with a glue-like sap. They do not try to hide the joins between the broken pieces but use a gold compound to highlight them, as in the image below. It is described at: https://traditionalkyoto.com/culture/kintsugi/

Some writers discuss whether Kintsugi is rooted in the beliefs of Japanese religions and this may be the case. But I believe that the ethos behind restoring broken pottery into something beautiful can be found in Christianity too.

Painting of an example of Japanese broken pottery repaired using the *Kintsugi* technique.

"Happy are those who are strong in the Lord. When they walk through the Valley of Weeping (the Valley of Baca), it will become a place of refreshing streams, where pools of blessing collect after the rains."
Psalm 84:5-6 (LB)

So many people's lives are shattered into many pieces by life's events and by others' cruelty and many people with broken lives come into our churches, to seek help. And I believe that, along with churches, Bethel Health & Healing Network and other caring Christian organisations, have a role to play in helping broken lives to be repaired, through our love and the healing power of the Holy Spirit. My own life has been repaired in this way and the lives of many people who have come to Bethel (and Gilgal and Jericho) have also been repaired, by helping them to put the pieces back together. Indeed, all three prophecy projects have helped people with broken lives; victims of domestic abuse (Gilgal), victims of modern slavery (Jericho) isolated pregnant women and others who are isolated or in great need (Bethel).

We live in a "blame the victim" culture and such victims are often blamed for the circumstances in which they find themselves. There is so much need for different non-judgmental approaches to help people in need. And the three prophecy projects, inspired by God alone, are right there at the coal face.

I feel so privileged that God first repaired me from my own trauma, and then used me, through the prophecy projects and through my own church, to help repair others with broken lives. That in itself has been healing. The gold that God brought into the cracks of my broken life included learning to forgive those who had wronged me; learning to control anger; finding an ability to stand alongside other broken people; intimacy with God; gradually becoming more obedient to God, and seeking to let the Fruits of the Spirit grow more in my life.

Love, Joy, Peace, Patience, Kindness, Goodness, Faithfulness, Gentleness and Self-Control. (Gal.5: 22).

And perhaps the greatest *gold* that God has placed in my life was to lead me into a contemplative prayer life, as described in my first book, "I Will Lift up my Eyes." A contemplative prayer life helps develop a close relationship with God, in which I have been able to commune with him, deep within myself, to find the way forward for my own life, in line with his plans for me.

> *"You can make many plans but the Lord's purpose will prevail"*
> Proverbs 19:21. (LB).

But, right up there, with all the Gold from God has been an opportunity to become an integral part of the three prophecy projects, which God brought to the inner city of Birmingham: Gilgal, Jericho and Bethel.

Also by Christine Parkinson

I will lift up my eyes (2001)

ISBN: 978-0-75520-047-4

This book will take you on a deep spiritual journey, whilst you travel with the author through the colourful cities of Kowloon, Manila, Singapore, Sydney, Bangkok and Calcutta, meeting on the way some significant Christian female pioneers of urban mission – Jackie Pullinger, Veronica Silva, Dorothy McMahon McCrae, Mother Teresa and others.

"A challenging and provoking book that will not leave you unmoved."

Available to order through all good bookshops or Internet bookstores or direct from the publisher at:
www.newgeneration-publishing.com

The Desert will Rejoice, Volume I (2004)

978-0-75520-113-6

Does God still speak to his people today, through prophetic words, pictures and dreams? Does he still inspire his followers to take certain actions, as he did in Biblical times? The author certainly believes so and, in this book, describes two prophecies given by different women about the city of Birmingham. The first prophecy told of "new beginnings" and gave the name for three God-inspired projects that would be set up in the city: Gilgal, Jericho and Bethel. This book tells the story of how they came to be set up and resourced, through a series of miraculous interventions, and of how they are now helping the most disadvantaged people in the city. It should encourage and inspire anybody with an interest in urban mission and those who believe that God is leading them in new directions.

Available to order through all good bookshops or Internet bookstores or direct from the publisher at:
www.newgeneration-publishing.com

Three Generations Left: human activity and the destruction of the planet (2016)

ISBN: 978-1-78719-041-2

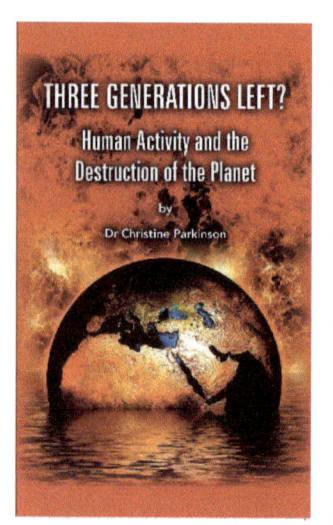

This book has been written in a simple, illustrated style, to encourage readers to understand what global warming and climate change are all about, why they are happening, and why there is a danger of the destruction of the planet within three generations (by the end of this century). It is really that serious but the media, hand in glove with the big corporations, continually plays it down.

Up to ten factors have all been working together to bring about the current situation and the book links them all together and shows how there needs to be a change from current thinking about the economy, growth and trade, if we are to save the planet.

Available to order through all good bookshops or Internet bookstores or direct from the publisher at:
www.newgeneration-publishing.com